Cute Little Ditty

Find Anything Wrong

AUTHOR: STEPHEN W. MILHOUSE

INSTRUCTIONS

Completely read the poem then go back and document any discrepancies, mistakes or illogical errors found on the blank pages provided at the end of the poem, in the special area provided in the ebook, or on a separate sheet of paper. See how close you can get to 25 or maybe you'll find some of the extra undocumented errors thrown in to test the person with exceptional attention to detail. This is a fun and educational challenge for people of all ages and educational backgrounds. Make it even more challenging by adding a time limit to reading and finding the errors. Example: See how many errors you can find in under 5 mins, 3 minutes or 2 minutes. Team up boys against the girls etc…

This boys and girls
is a cute <u>little ditty</u>

about a pig, a horse, a cow and a kitty

The pig's name was "Portly"
The horse was called "Helen"
The cow's was named "Courtney"
The kitty called "Ellen

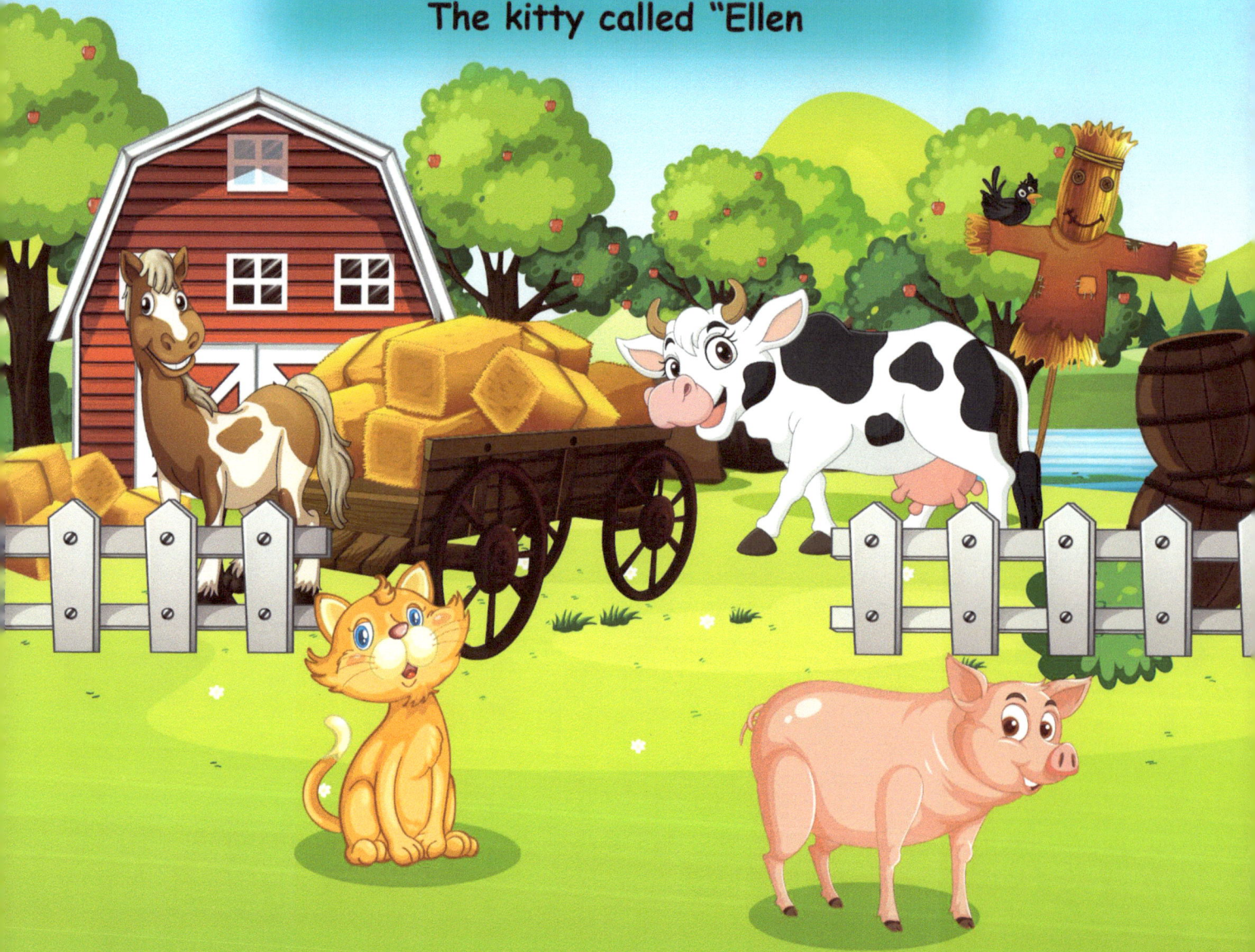

they all lived together
safe from all harm
on one hundred ten acres
called "The Anderson's Farm"

THE
ANDERSON'S
FARM

One dark sunny night
while sleeping awake
Portly the horse
lost a terrible mistake

THE
ANDERSON'S
FARM

Things just weren't right in the
world as he new it
so she went to ask Cortney
but somehow she blue it

Portley? she asked in the day of the night
something is rong can u help
make it all right

Courtney the kitty said with a grin
sorry can't help you
go ask "Helen the hen

So she went to ask Helen
but was found on the way
by Courtney the pig
and a duck eating hay

I no where I am
Helen said with a smile
If we keep walking straight
we'll be there in awhile

So they walked in a circle
shaped like a hook
and in moments arrived
at a pond by a brook

the lake was reel small
and covered with sand
Helen exclaimed very softly
I know where I am

and at that just moment
Helen woke with a scream
you see boys and girls
this was all just a dream

THE
ANDERSON'S
FARM

THE END

NUMBER AND WRITE YOUR CORRECTIONS HERE

_____

_____

_____

_____

_____

_____

NUMBER AND WRITE YOUR CORRECTIONS HERE

NUMBER AND WRITE YOUR CORRECTIONS HERE

NUMBER AND WRITE YOUR CORRECTIONS HERE

_____

_____

_____

_____

_____

NUMBER AND WRITE
YOUR CORRECTIONS HERE

_____

_____

_____

_____

_____

_____

NUMBER AND WRITE
YOUR CORRECTIONS HERE

_____

_____

_____

_____

_____

"CUTE LITTLE DITTY"
[FIND ANYTHING WRONG]
CORRECTION SHEET 25 OR MORE FOUND

This boys and girls
is a cute little ditty
about a pig
a horse
a cow and
a kitty

The pig's name was "Portly"
The horse was called "Helen"
The cow's was named "Courtney"
The kitty called "Ellen"

t~~hey~~ all lived together {capital T}
safe from all harm
on one hundred ten acres
called "The Anderson's Farm"

One ~~dark sunny night~~ {dark sunny}
while ~~sleeping awake~~ {sleeping awake}
~~Portly~~ the horse {Portly was the pig}
~~lost~~ a terrible mistake {lost s/b made}

"CUTE LITTLE DITTY" [FIND ANYTHING WRONG]

CORRECTION SHEET 25 OR MORE FOUND

Things just weren't right in the world
as he ~~new~~ it {new s/b{knew}
so ~~she~~ went to ask Cortney {she s/b he}
but somehow ~~she blue~~ it {she s/b he} {blue s/b blew}

Portley~~? she~~ asked in the ~~day of the night~~ {she s/b he}{he was Portly and
Portley is misspelled} {day of the night}{,missing}{?}
something is ~~rong~~ can ~~u~~ help make it all right {s/b wrong {u s/b you} & missing ?}

~~Courtney the kitty~~ said with a grin {Courtney is the cow}{, after kitty/grin}
sorry can't help you {s/b "Sorry can't help you}
go ask "~~Helen the hen~~ {Helen is the horse}{missing . closing quotation}

So she went to ask Helen
but was found on the way
by ~~Courtney the pig~~ {Courtney s/b the cow}
and a ~~duck eating hay~~ {Ducks don't eat hay. A horse eats hay}

I ~~no~~ where I am {no s/b know}
Helen said with a smile
If we keep walking straight
we'll be there in awhile

"CUTE LITTLE DITTY"
[FIND ANYTHING WRONG]
CORRECTION SHEET 25 OR MORE FOUND

So they walked in a ~~circle~~
~~shaped like a hook~~ {a circle can't be shaped like a hook}
and in moments arrived
at a pond by a brook

~~the lake was reel small~~ {lake was originally a pond}{reel s/b real}
and ~~covered with sand~~ {no body of water can be covered with sand}
Helen ~~exclaimed very softly~~ {exclaim means to cry out loudly}
I know where I am

~~and at that just moment~~ {s/b And}{s/b and just at that moment}
Helen woke with a scream
you see boys and girls
this was all just a ~~dream~~ {if she woke with a scream she was having a nightmare not a dream}

The End
©By: Stephen W. Milhouse
November 06, 1998

www.ingramcontent.com/pod-product-compliance
Lightning Source LLC
Chambersburg PA
CBHW061357090426
42739CB00003B/49